DAG NABBIT

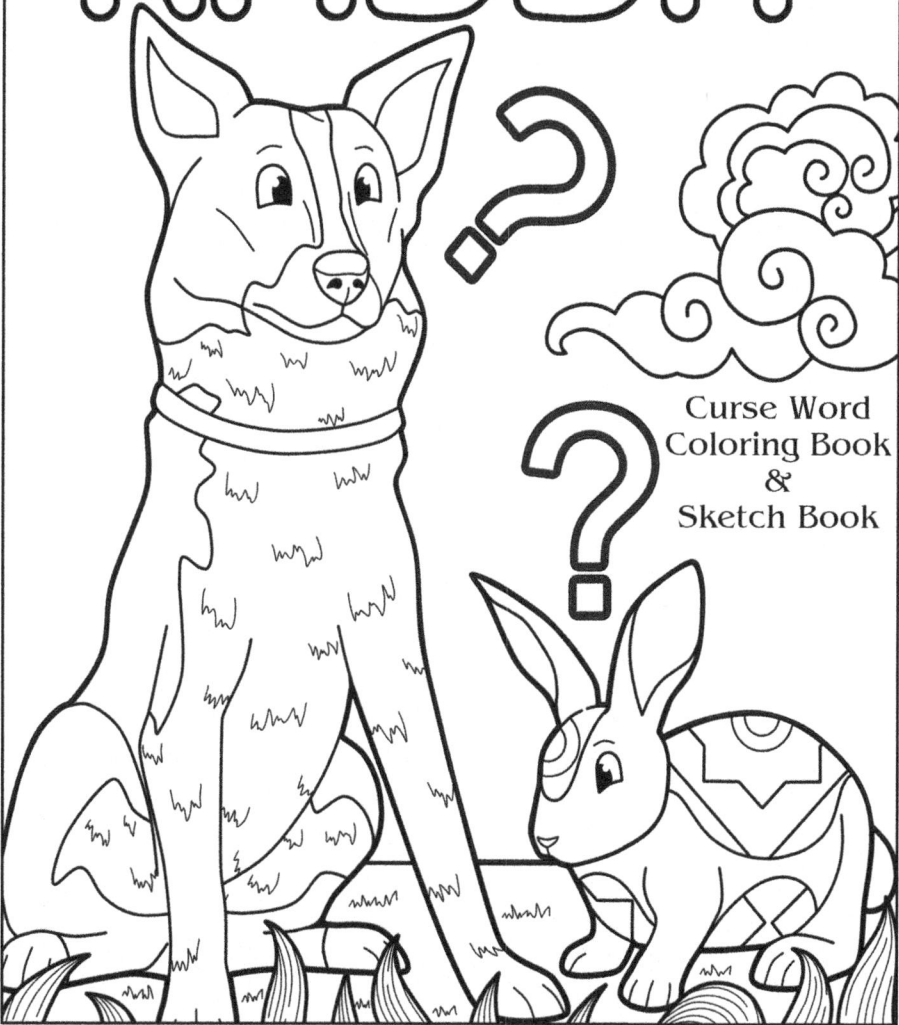

Curse Word
Coloring Book
&
Sketch Book

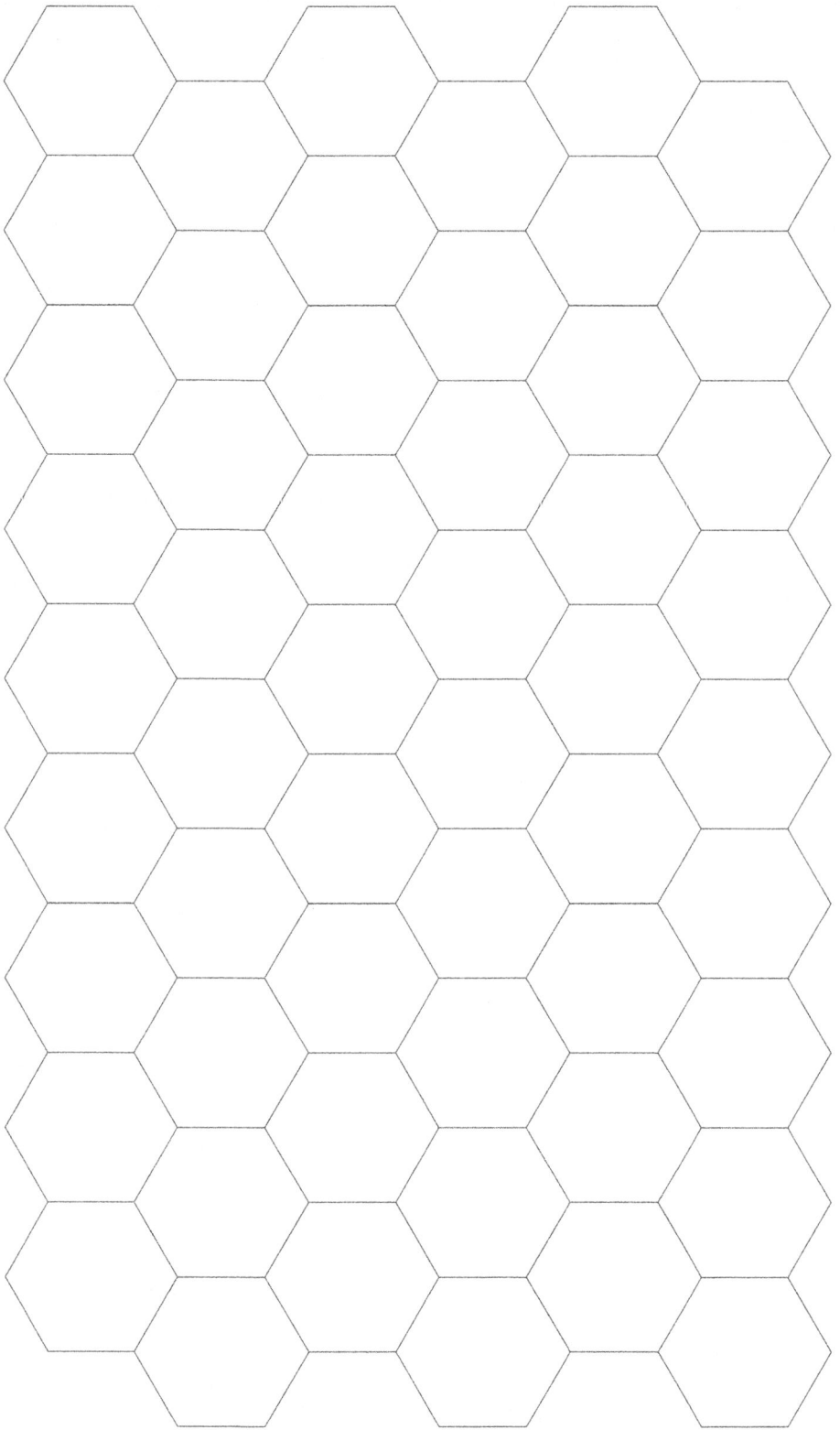

Bless their Little Hearts

Contributed by Fairlee Corkran

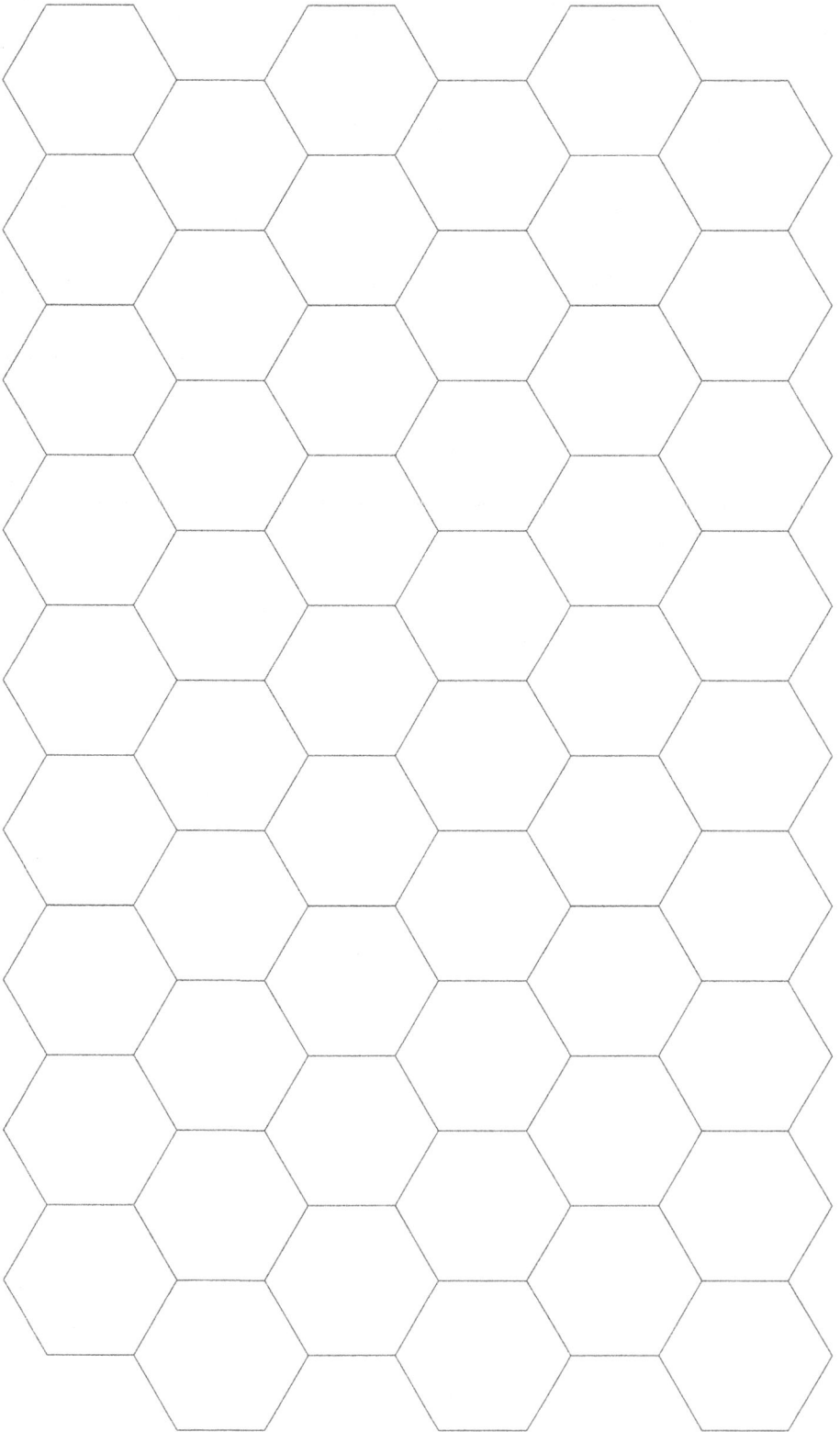

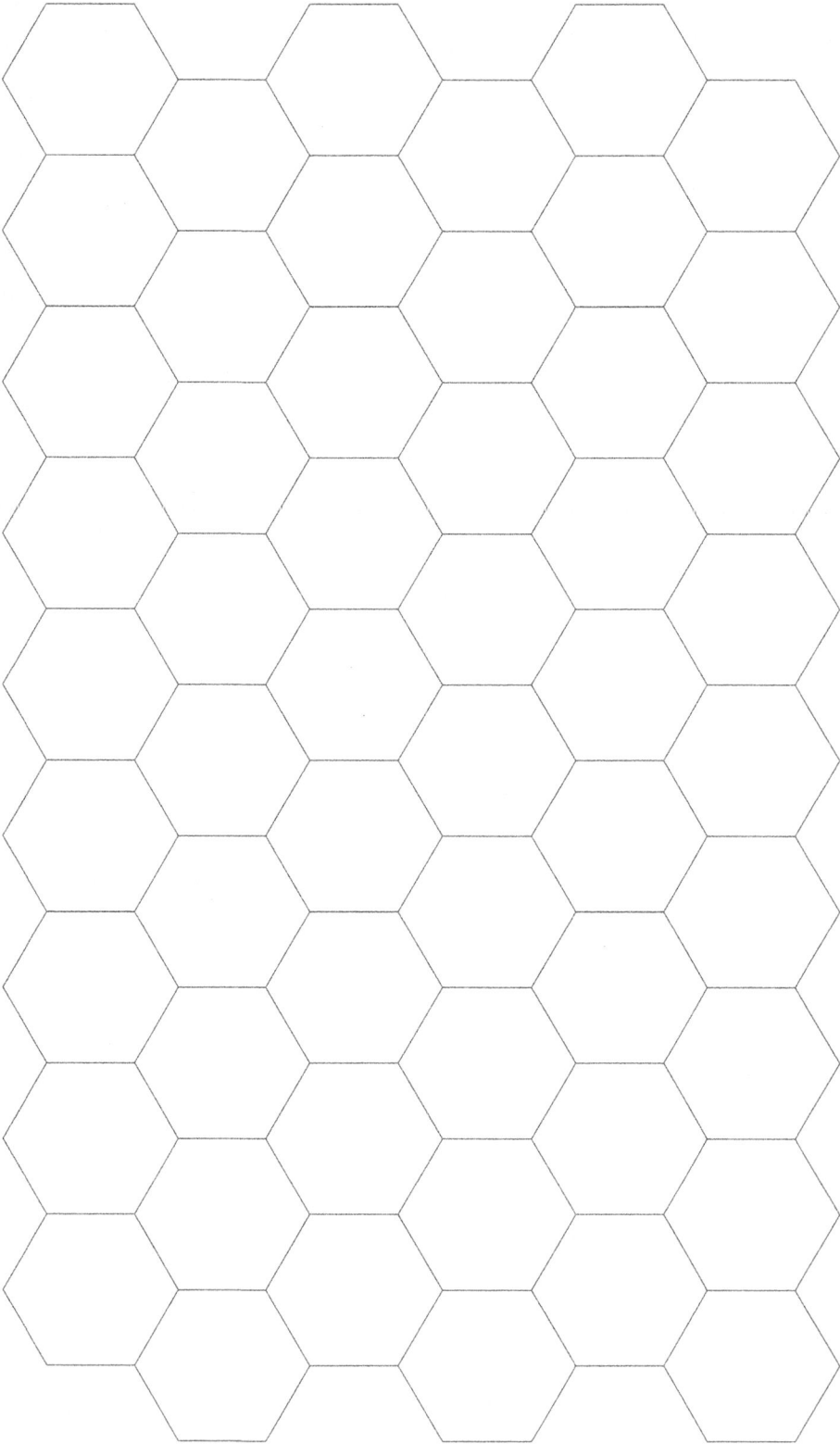

DARN TOOTEN

Contributed by Samantha Tomilson

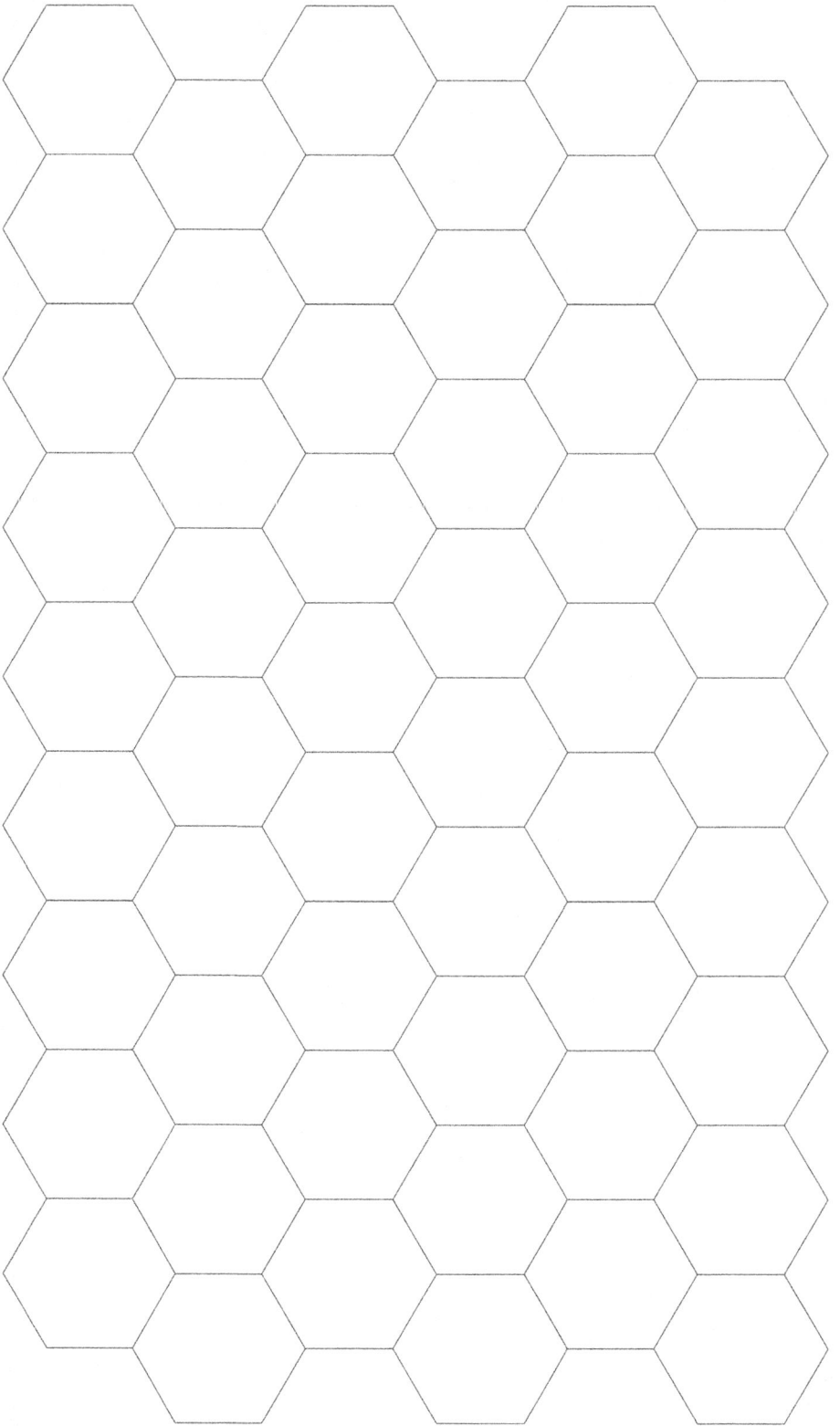

Dog Gone It!

Contributed by Kim Forthofer

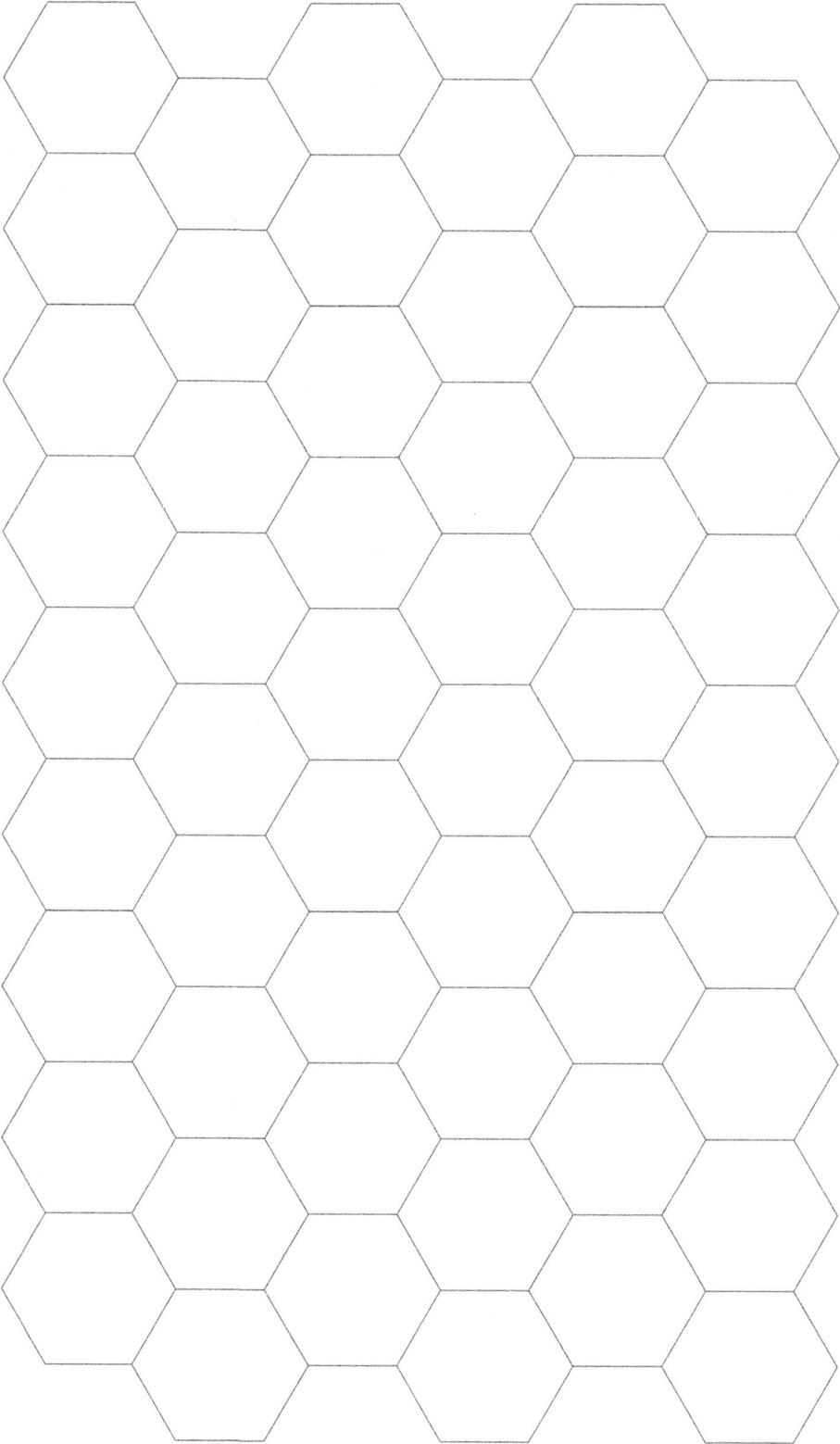

FLUFFY MUFFIN PANTS

CONTRIBUTED BY TESSA JOHNSON

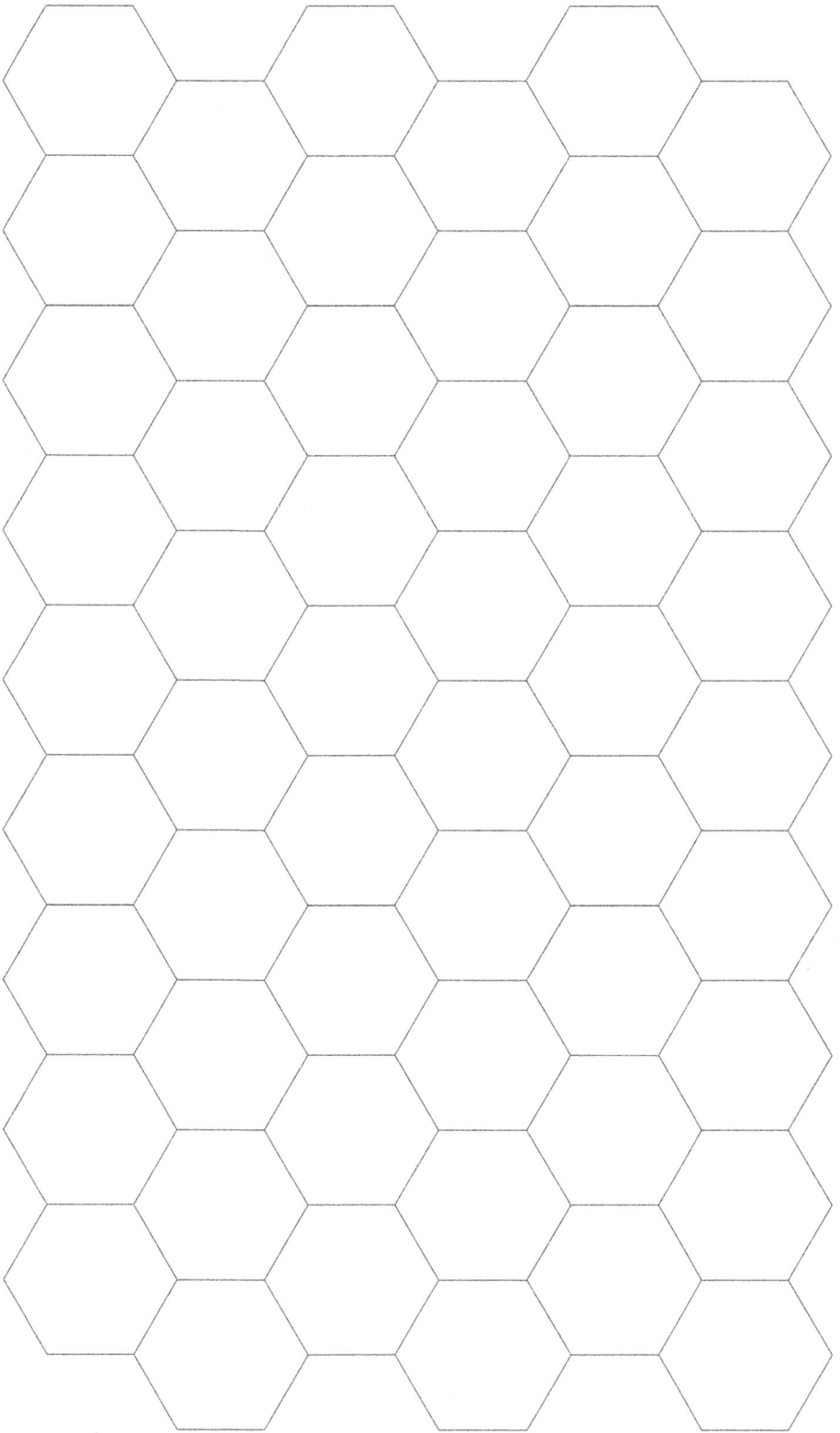

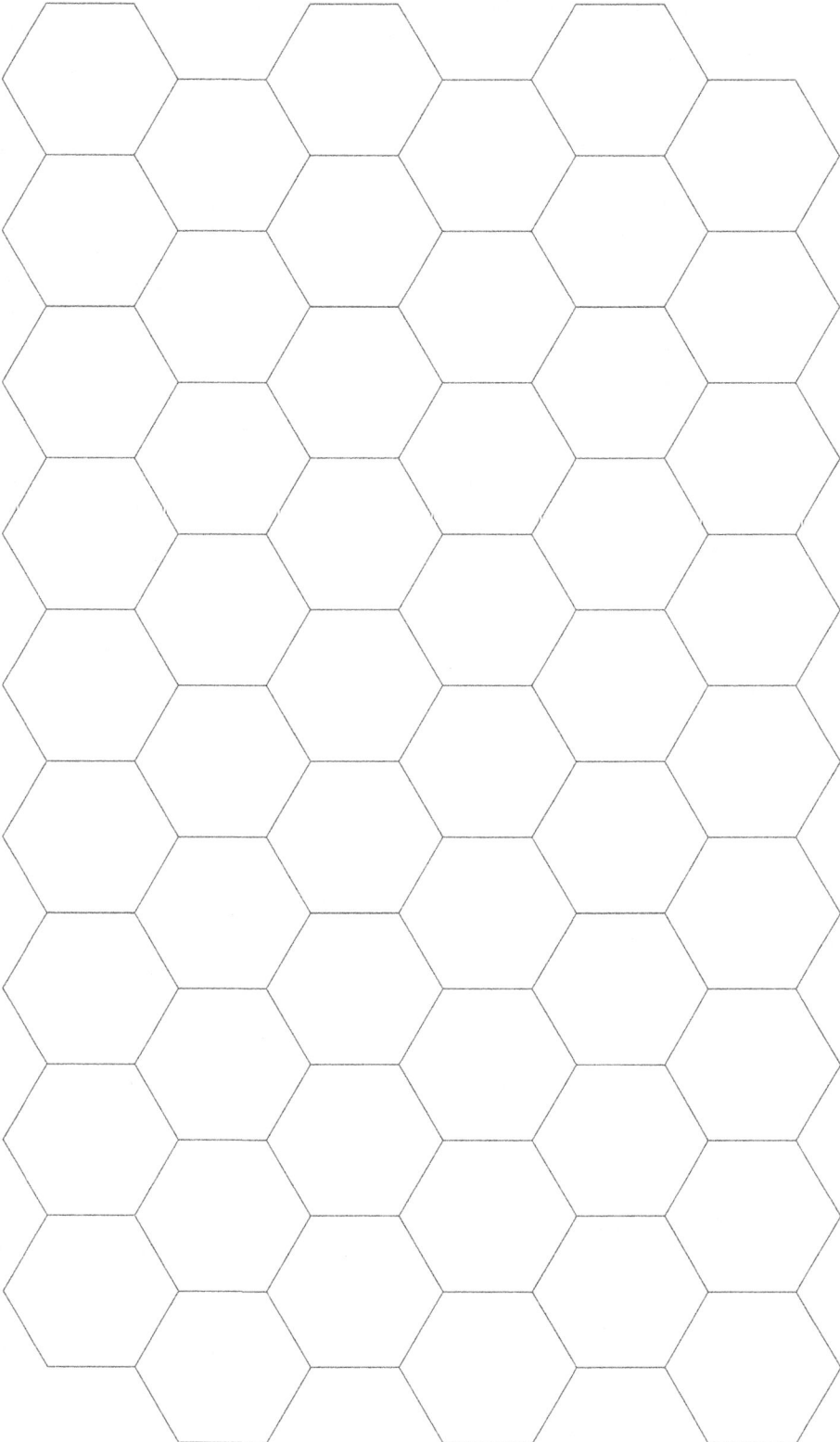

For the LOVE of Pete!

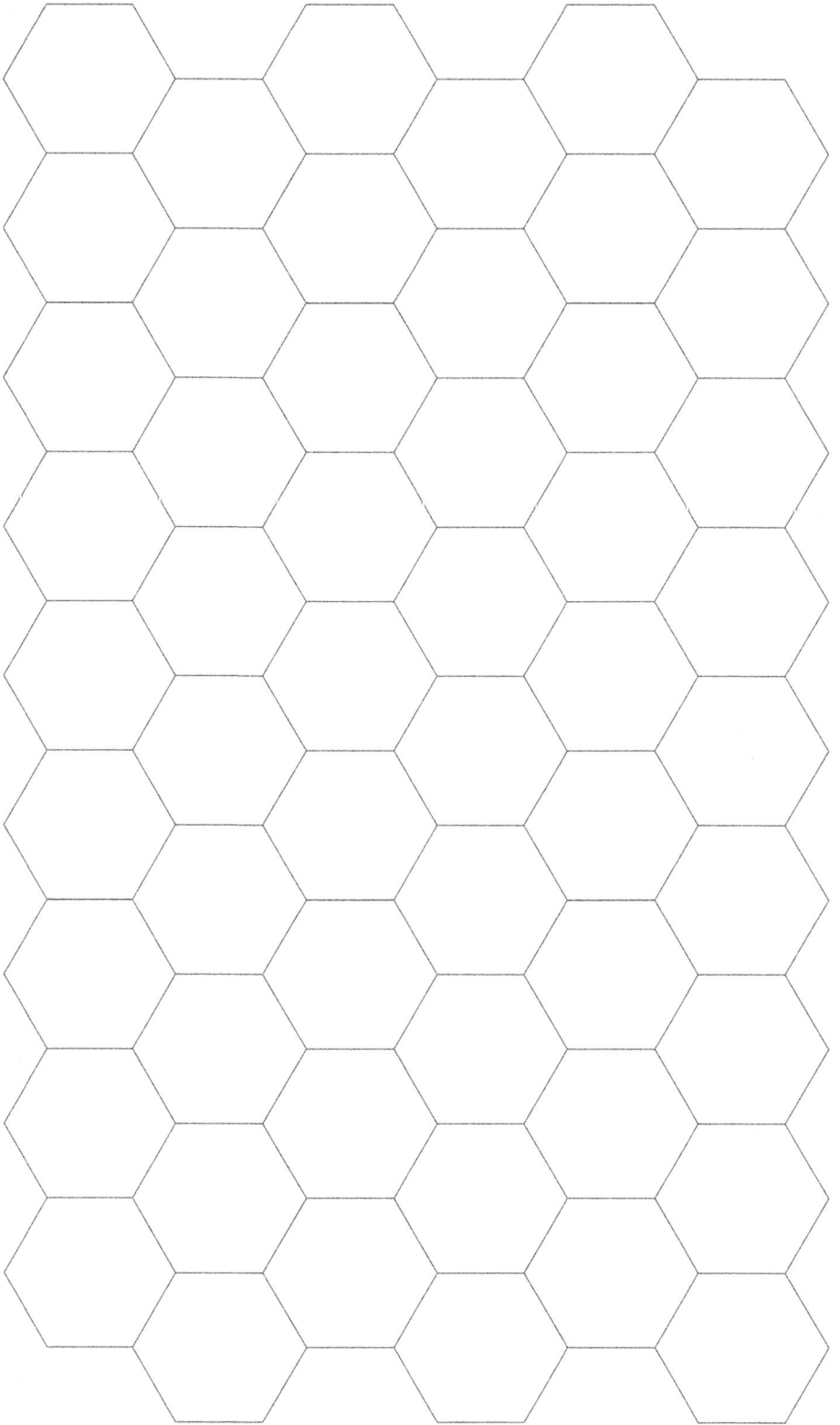

hasenpfeffen

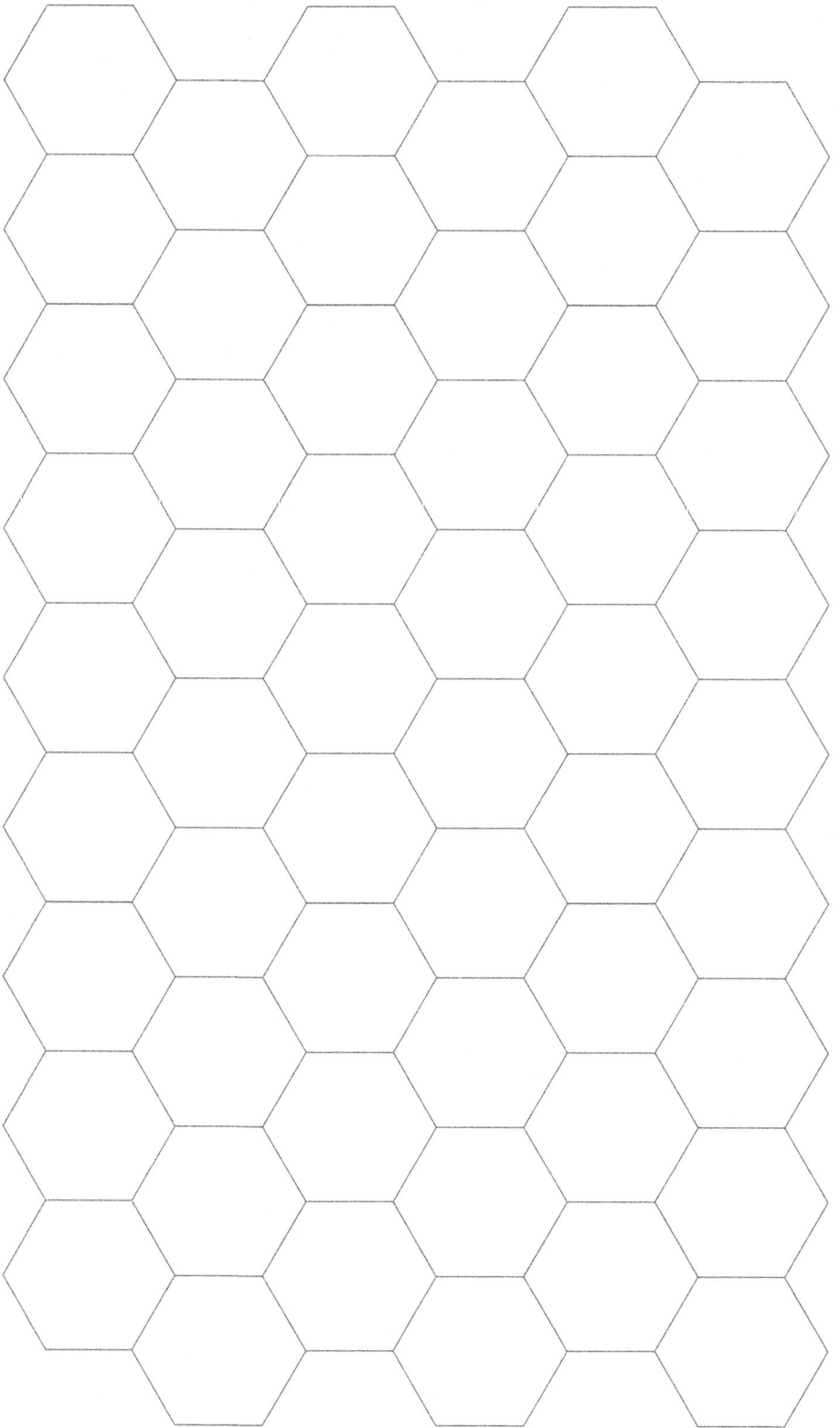

HORSE
HOCKEY

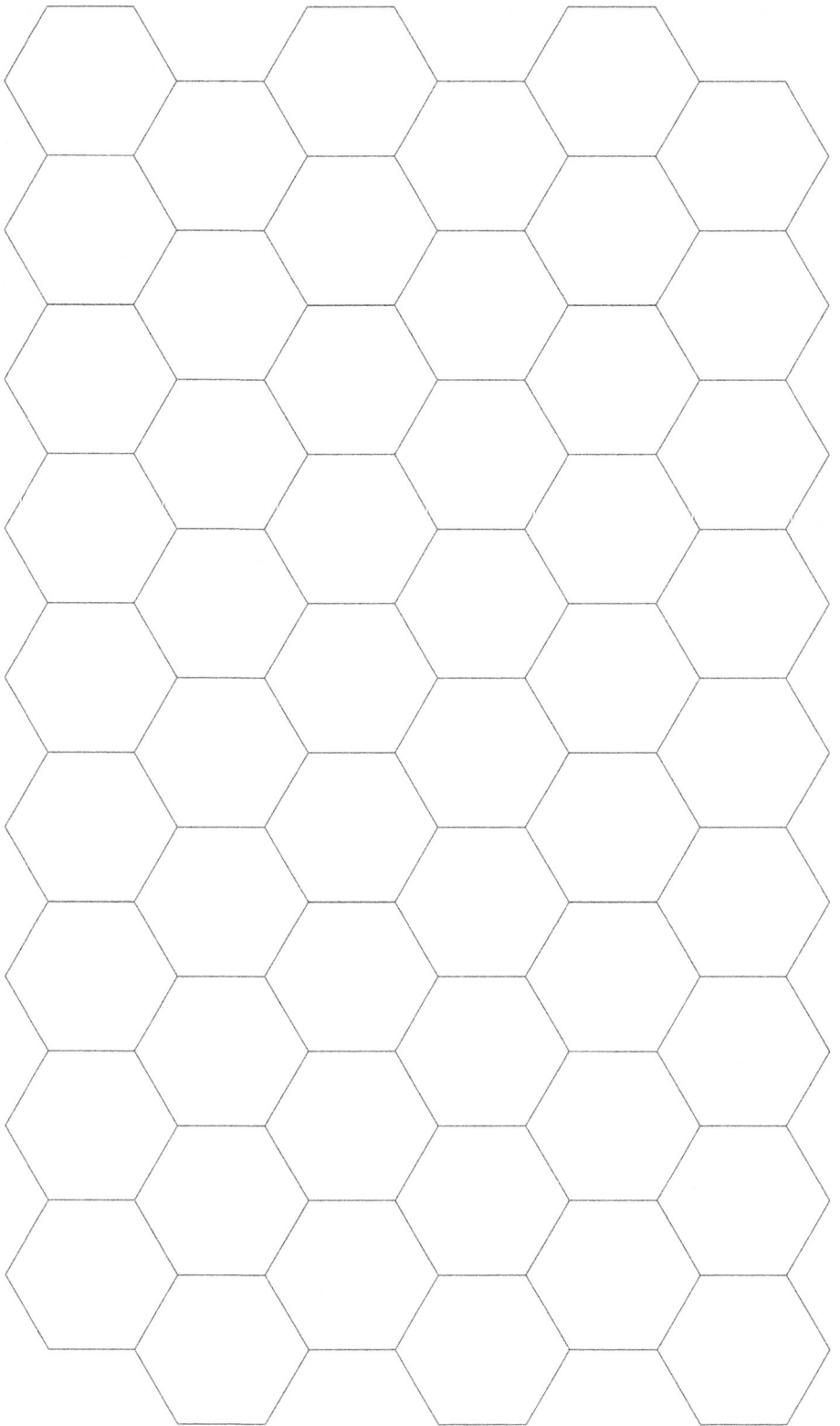

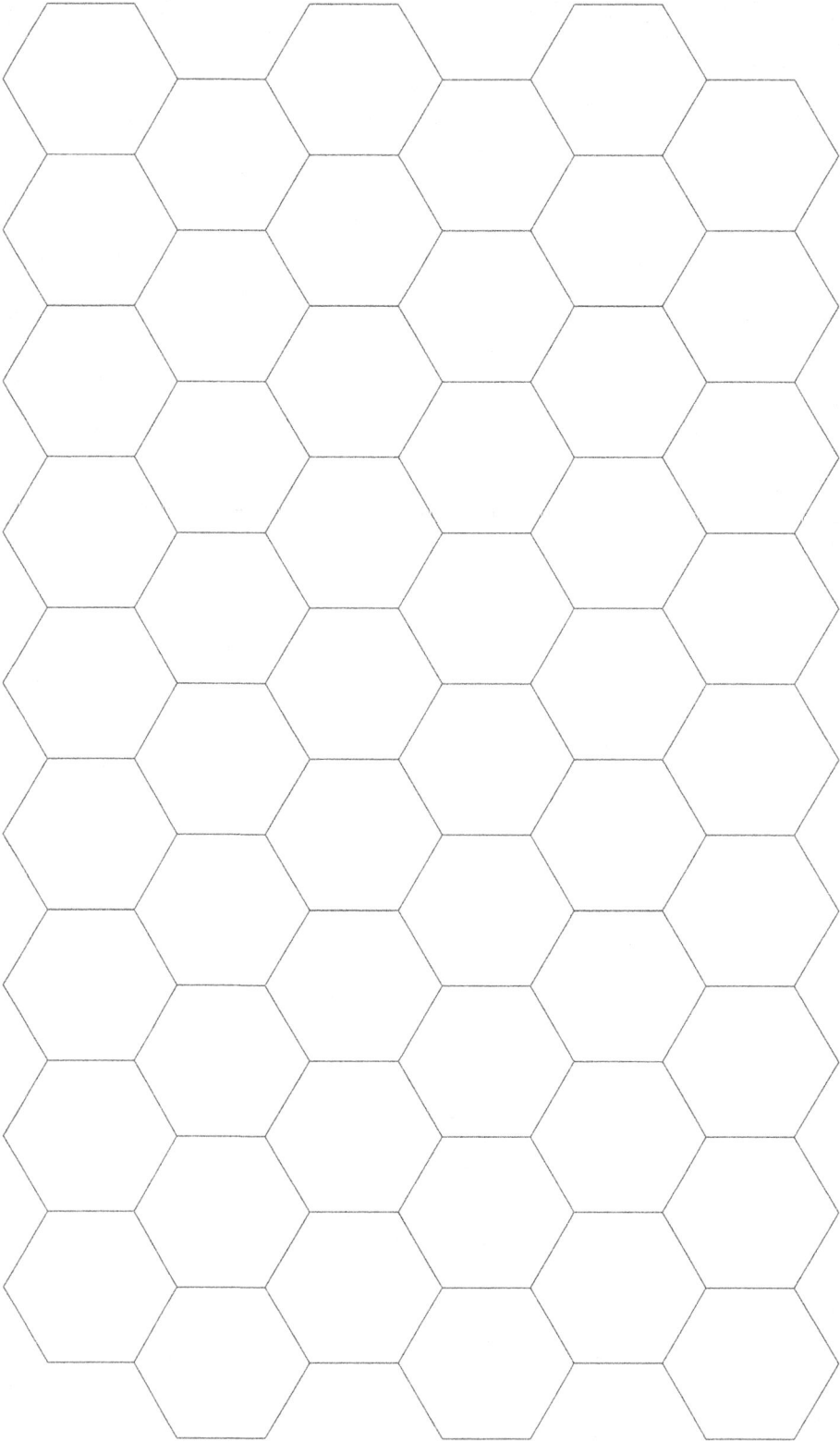

MOTHER OF PEARL!

Contributed by Rayven Monique

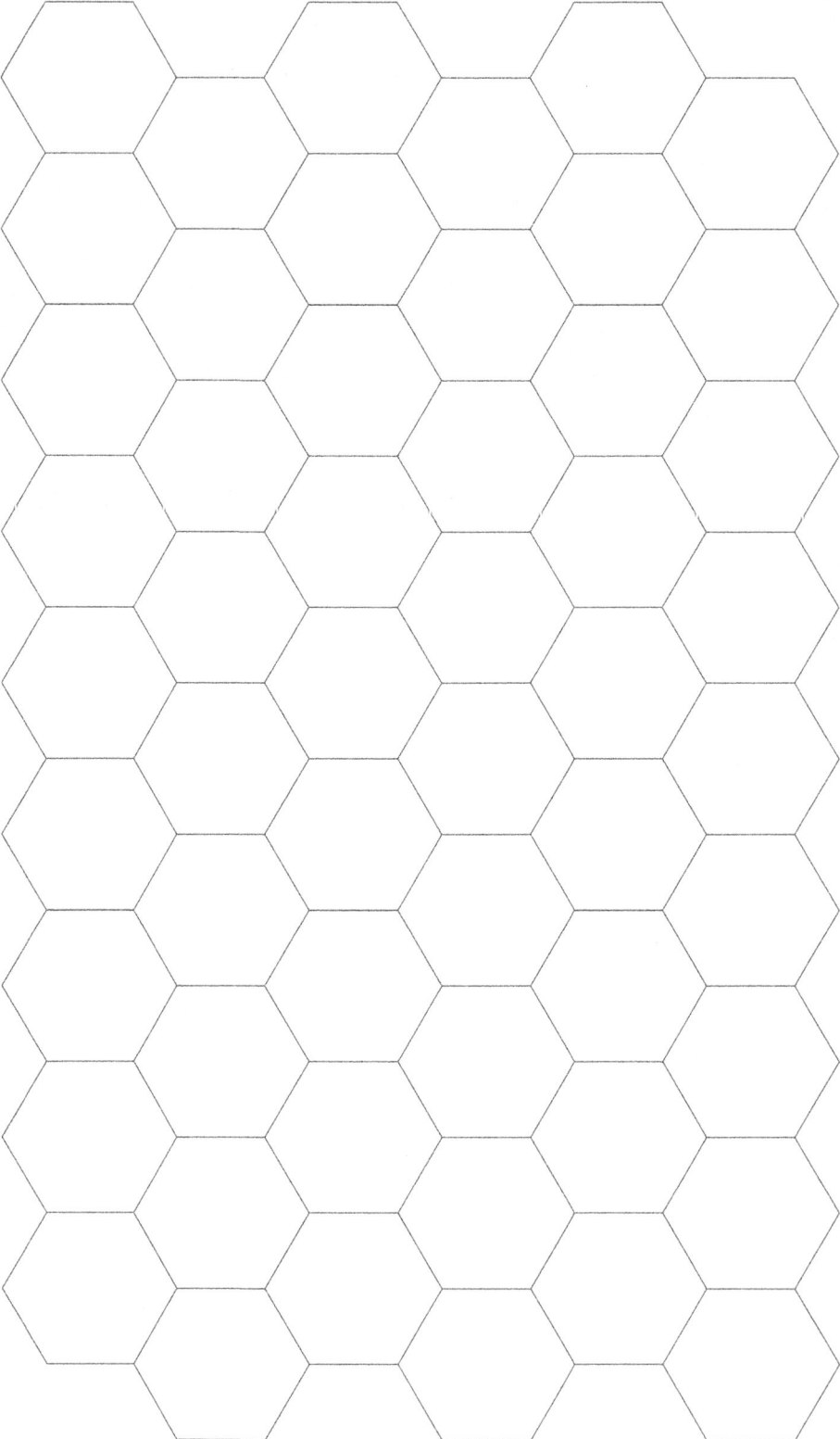

Contributed by:
Pam Boik

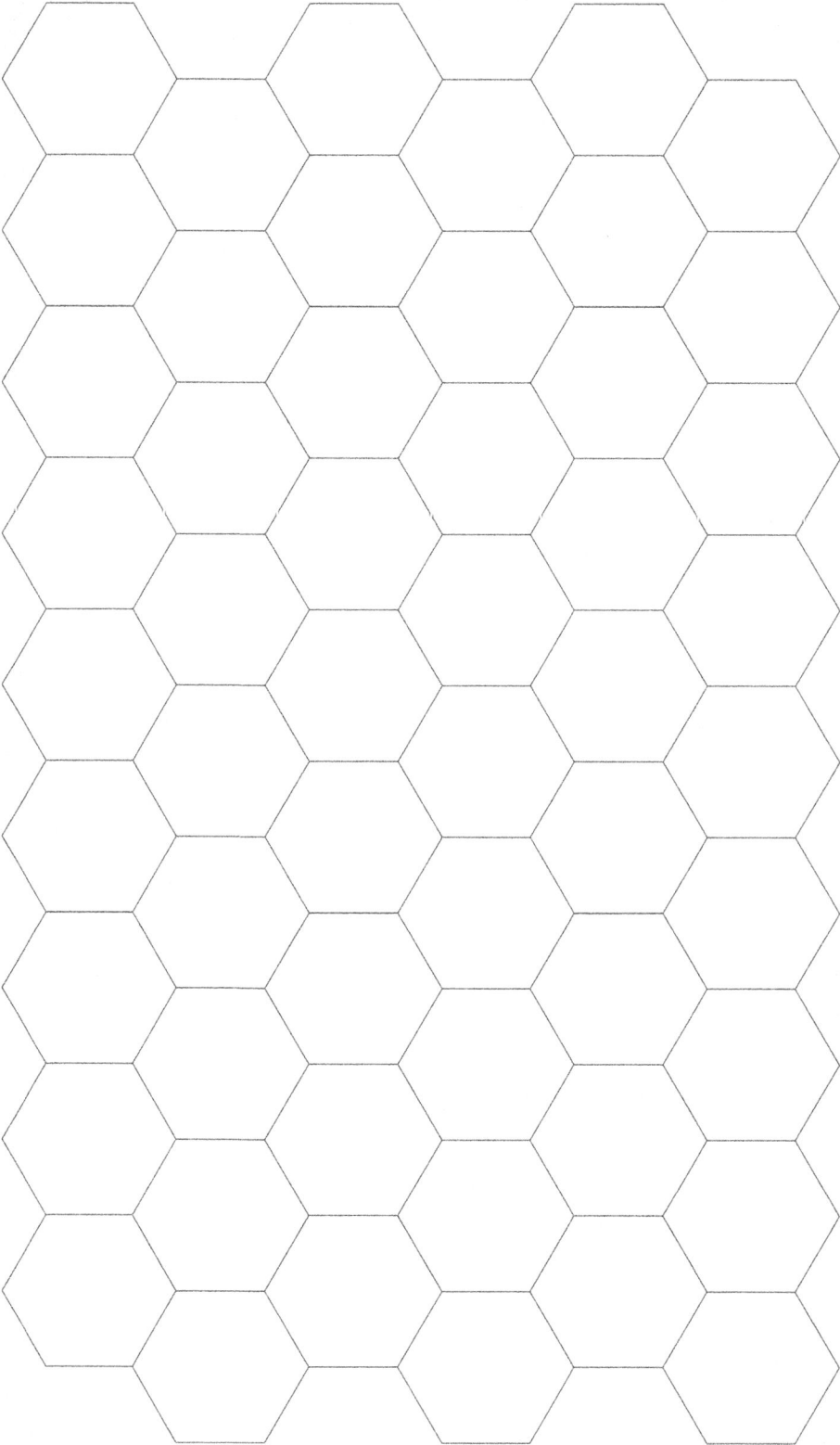

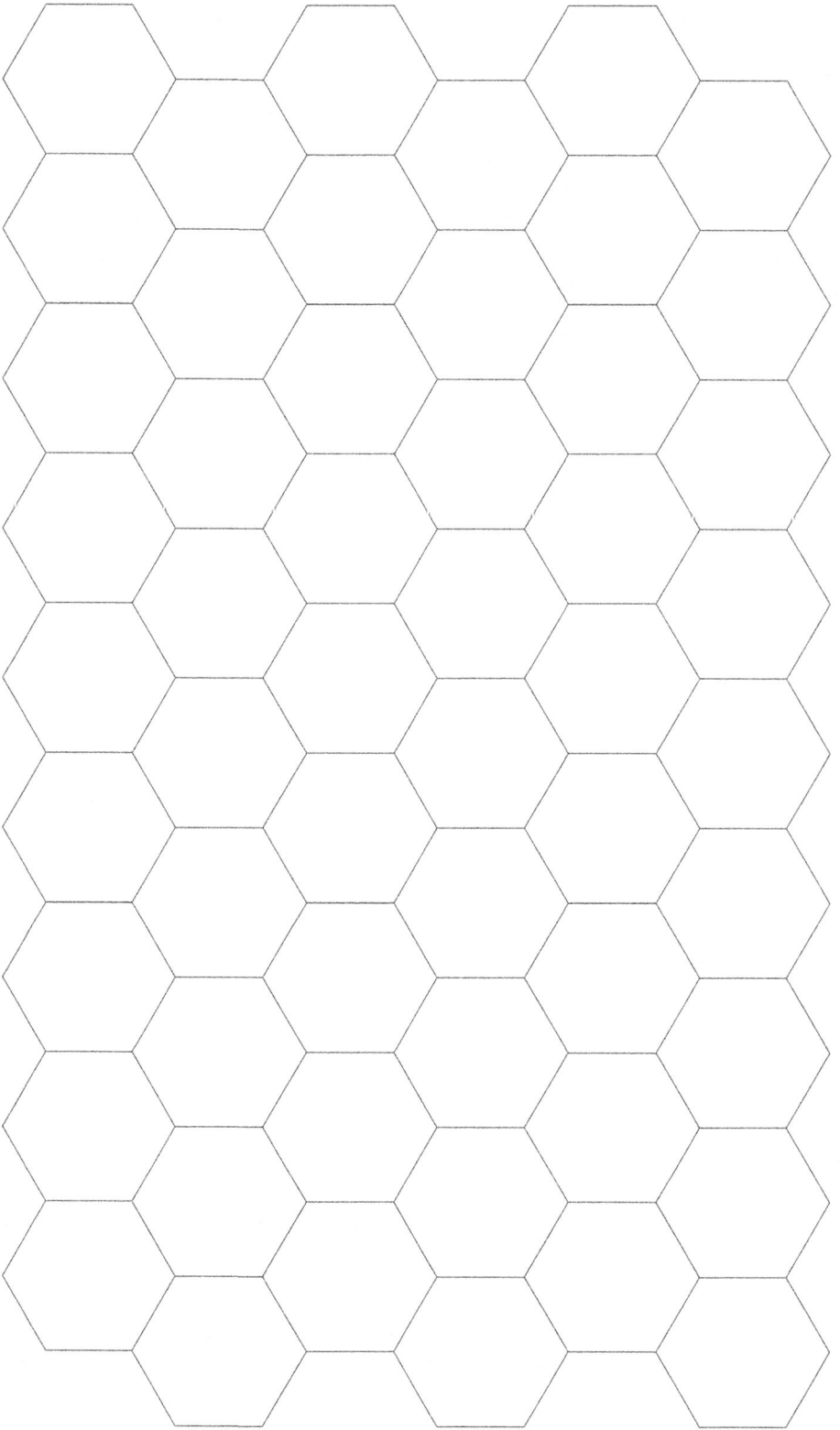

CONTRIBUTED BY STEPHANIE KALINEC

PUSS N' BOOTS

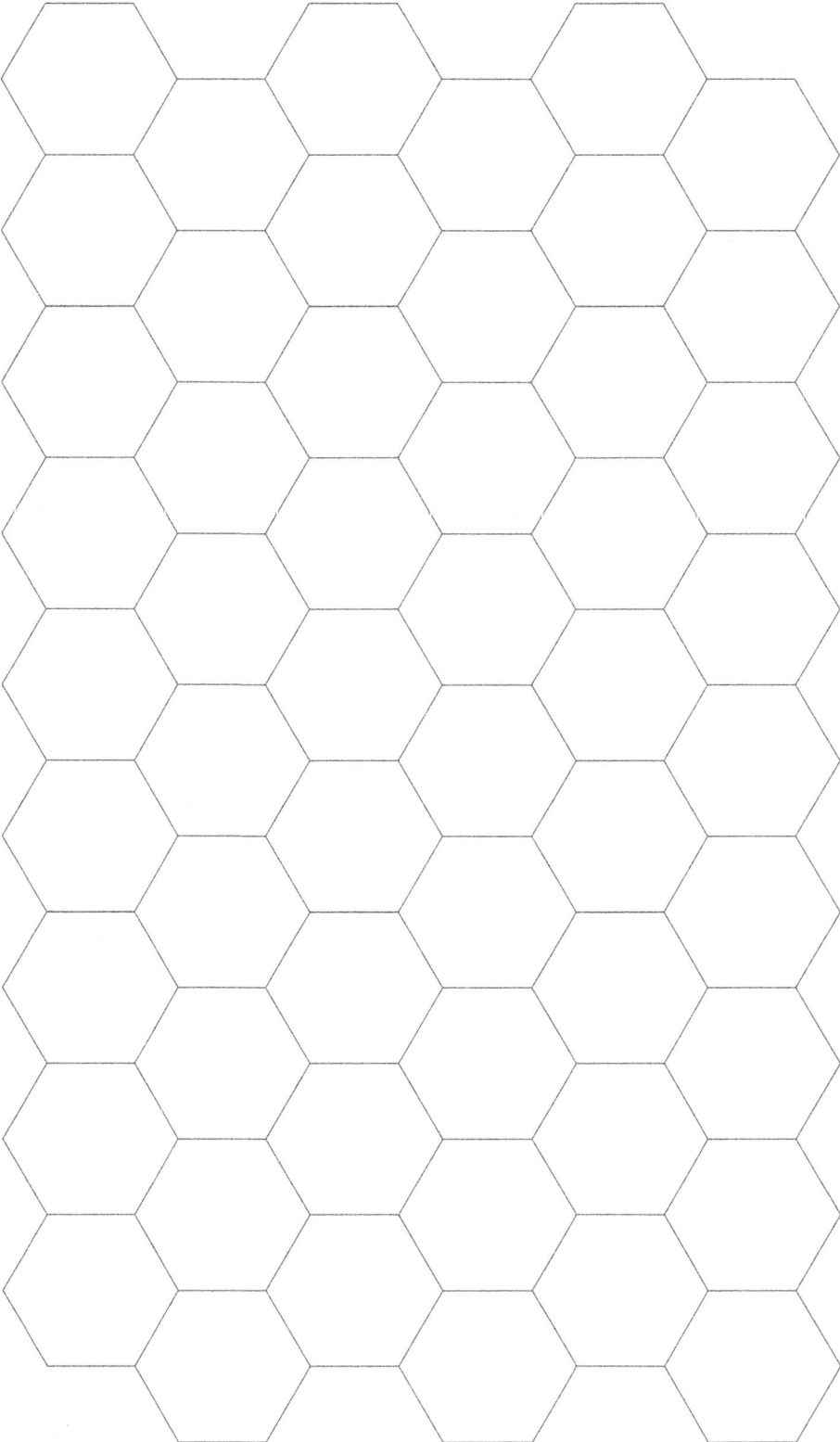

SON OF A BIG BLUE BIRD!

Contributed by:
Ronda Davis-Riehl

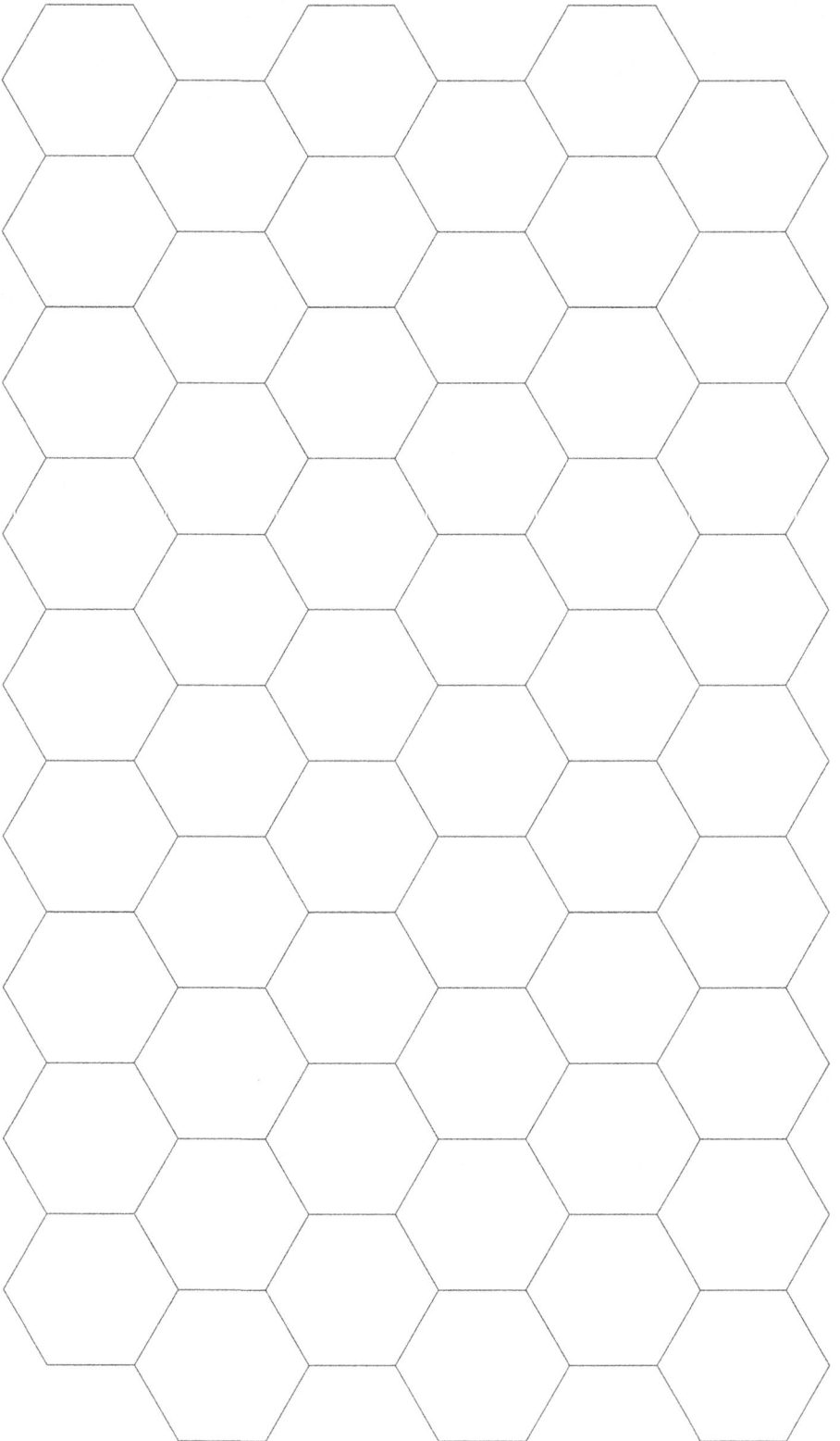

Got Dandruff, some of it Itches!

Contributed by Sara Gray

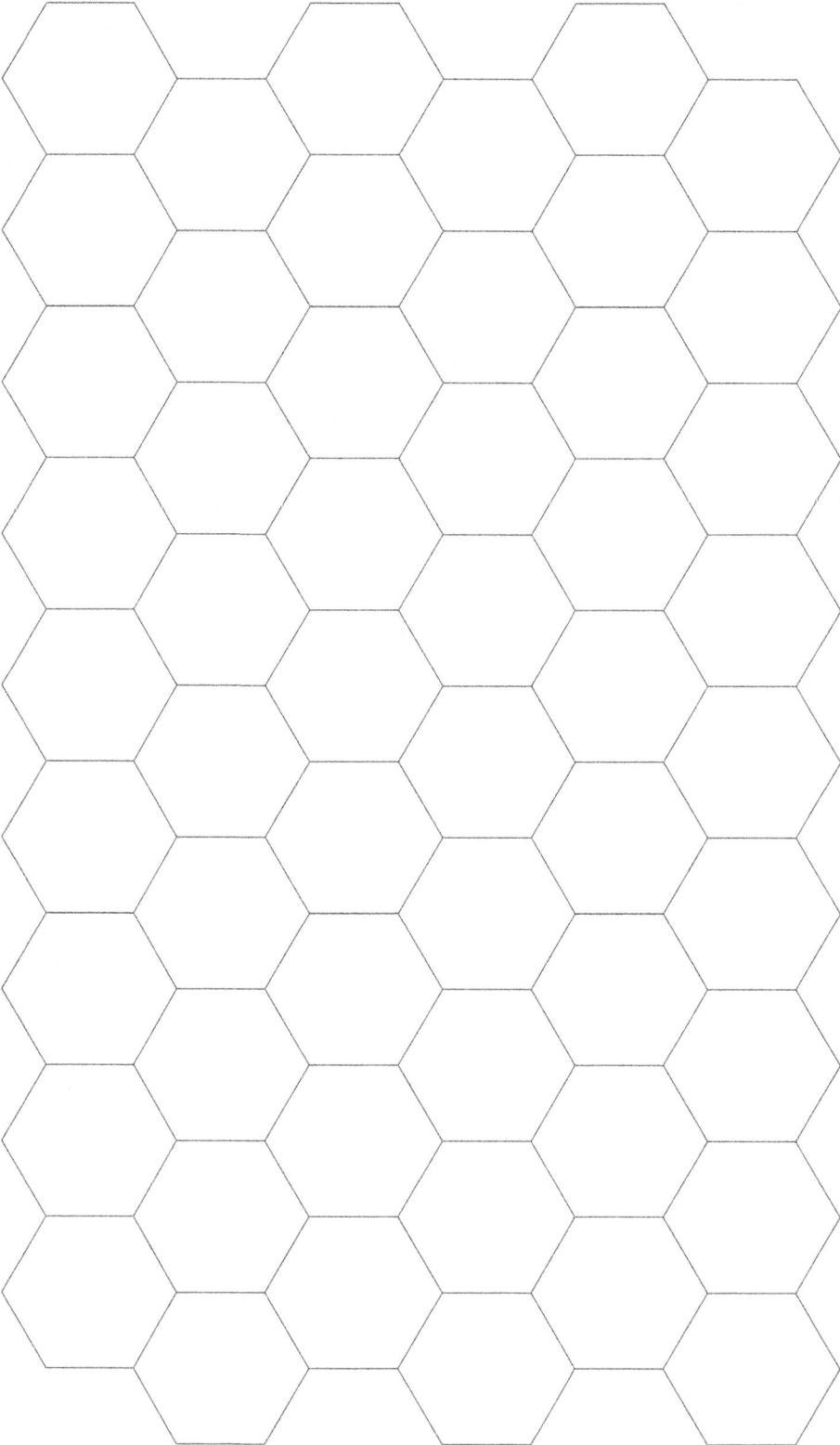

Wicked

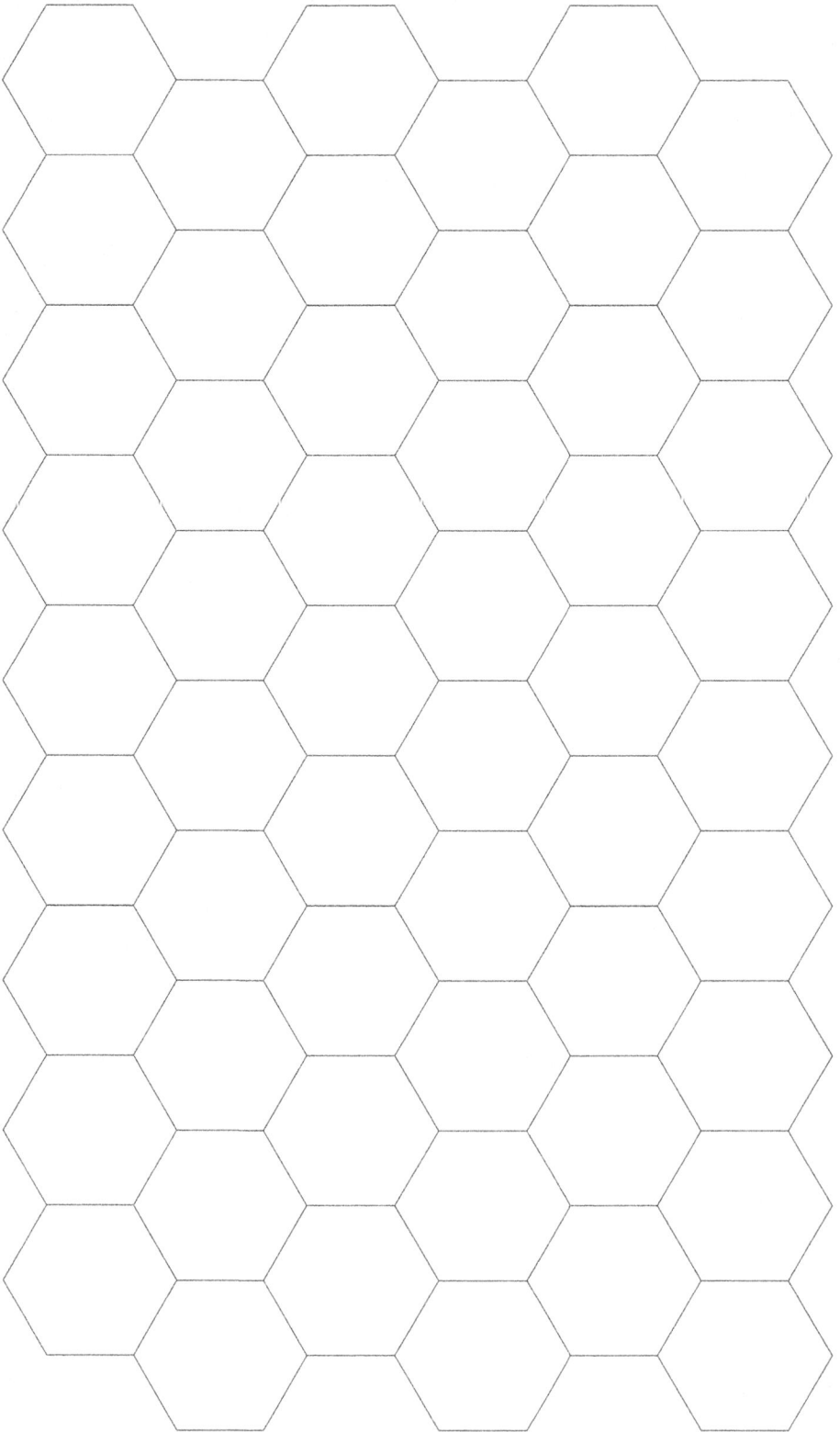

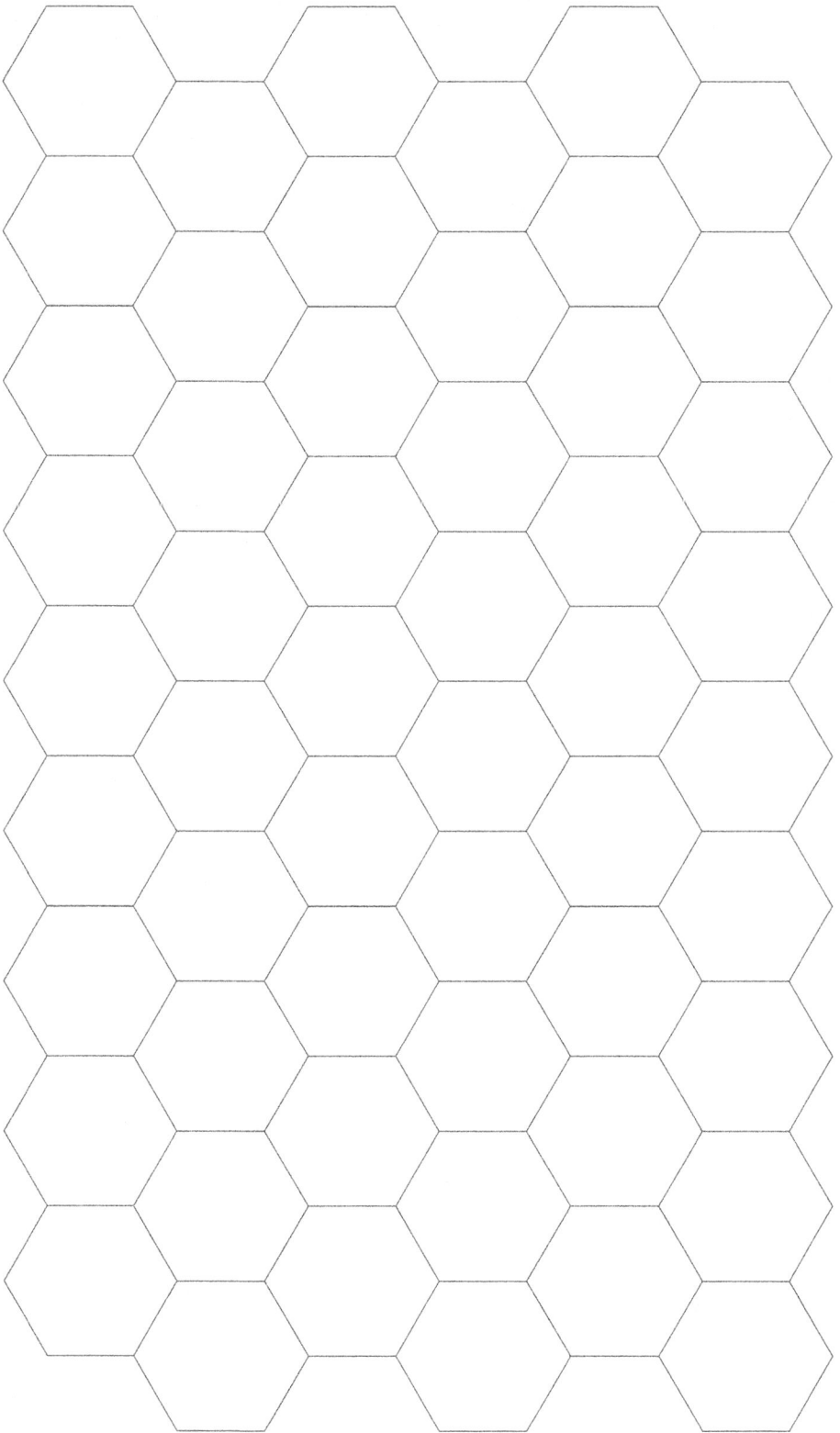

GET YOUR FREE
COLORING BOOK

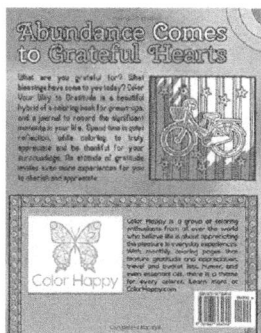

Bonus Compassion Cards

YOU ARE ENOUGH

THANK YOU

Have a WONDERFUL DAY

YOU ARE SPECIAL

olor Happy ®, we are on a quest to spread joy and happiness through color. Each month our Butterflies (our fun word members") from all over the world color and pass out Compassion Cards to family members, friends, acquaintances, even strangers, in an effort to make the world a little brighter. We would be honored to have you join us in this quest by ading a little love yourself.

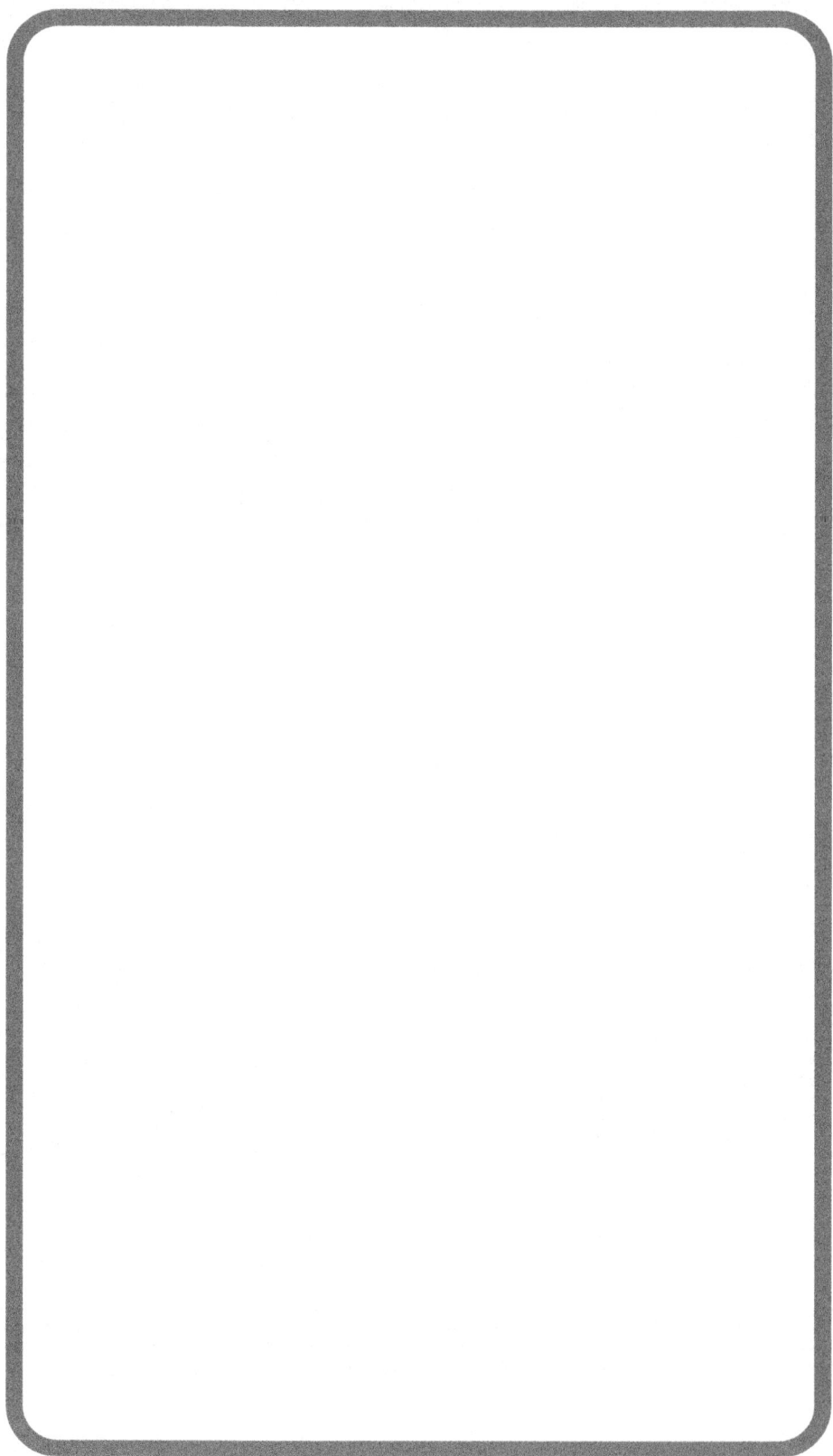

Made in the USA
Las Vegas, NV
18 August 2021